Original title:
Under the Same Roof, Apart

Copyright © 2025 Creative Arts Management OÜ
All rights reserved.

Author: Milo Harrington
ISBN HARDBACK: 978-1-80587-090-6
ISBN PAPERBACK: 978-1-80587-560-4

Fragile Connections

In the kitchen, I find your socks,
They dance with crumbs like little rocks.
Our cat sits proud, a royal scout,
While I'll just sip, unsure, no doubt.

The fridge makes noise, a little whale,
It hums our tales of love and fail.
You watch your show, I steal your snacks,
Together lost, yet never tracks.

Empty Room Conversations

With each bold laugh, you summon light,
Yet here we are, both out of sight.
I talk to plants; they nod their heads,
While you're deep in dreams, on cozy beds.

The echo of footsteps, a comical chase,
It feels like we dance in our own space.
I ask the couch, 'What's on your mind?'
It just sits there, eternally blind.

Moments Between Heartbeats

The clock ticks loud, an impatient friend,
Each second stretched, does it ever end?
I glance at you, a half-sleepy face,
Hard to connect in this cozy place.

You steal the blankets, I take a sigh,
We're peaceful chaos, you and I.
In the rush of beats, we grin, we tease,
Finding joy in discord, a rare breeze.

Fraying Threads of Union

Your shoelaces tie themselves in knots,
A pallid fashion, but who cares a lot?
You drip your coffee, and I spill my tea,
Yet here we are, in this comedy.

The Wi-Fi flickers, our screens reset,
I argue with my phone; it's not a threat.
We share this giggle, absurd but true,
In tangled threads, I still find you.

Moments of Connection

In the kitchen, you're making a mess,
While I'm dodging dishes, I must confess.
We laugh over crumbs, a flour fight,
Dinner's late, but the mood is right.

You steal my snacks when I look away,
I plot my revenge for another day.
In this dance of mischief, we find our groove,
Both loving and hating, but always in tune.

Love Between the Cracks

You stack your shoes high, I call it a tower,
I can't find my socks that were here just an hour.
Yet every cluttered corner tells our tale,
Of love that survives in chaos without fail.

You hide the remote, I feign despair,
But your laughter brings warmth to the chilly air.
Our quirks intertwine in a silly ballet,
Creating a bond that's quirky and gay.

Glances Through the Doorway

I see you stealing a sip from my drink,
You wink at me, as if making me think.
With a smile so bright, like a cheeky spark,
But you'll trip over shoes left in the dark.

Our eyes lock in secret shared glee,
When you steal my fries, that's a victory!
In these playful skirmishes, laughter's our song,
Together alone, where we both belong.

Unraveled Threads of Affection

Our laundry piles up like a colorful hill,
Each shirt a memory, a love that won't chill.
Yet when you steal my favorite old tee,
I can't help but laugh, oh, just let it be!

You've got your quirks, I've got mine too,
Who knew that chaos could feel so true?
In this tangled mess, we find our grace,
Sewn together by laughter in this shared space.

Windows to Our Isolation

Through glassy panes we stare,
As life's absurdity hangs in air.
Neighbors wave, but we don't meet,
Just laugh at quirks from our own seats.

Cats play king on their own thrones,
While we're way too cozy with our phones.
Coffee brews, but we're not in line,
One's out of puns, the other's out of wine.

Invisible Barriers in Familiarity

We share a wall, though worlds apart,
Your loud TV is a work of art.
I sing off-key to drown your shouts,
Our love's a dance with silly doubts.

You've got a broom, it's lost its way,
Mine's a wand for a laundry ballet.
Together we brave the grocery run,
But in the aisle, it's all just fun.

Hearts in Different Time Zones

You rise with roosters, I sleep with dreams,
Our schedules wobble in funny schemes.
You text me brunch, it's late for tea,
While I bake cookies for my lonely spree.

A card game ends with not a score,
As we toss chips like we're at war.
I'll trade you tales from dusk till dawn,
Through silly laughter, our worries are gone.

The Space Between Us

You've got your snacks, I've got mine too,
We cheer for champions we never knew.
Dance parties break with a single song,
Separated cheers, but man, they're strong.

Your laugh's a wave, my sigh's a breeze,
We're together while doing as we please.
So here's to the fun in our little lair,
With silly antics filling up the air.

The Invisible Thread Between Us

In the kitchen, I stir the pot,
You watch from the couch, lost in thought.
Your socks are clean, yet somehow unmatched,
Like our conversations, a bit detached.

You laugh at my jokes, though you roll your eyes,
I borrow your shirts, to wear with surprise.
In this funny dance, we twirl and we spin,
Sharing a space, yet we each have our skin.

Partitioned Lives

Our fridge is a battle of flavors so bold,
You stick with your yogurt, I crave something cold.
The remote is a prize, won in a scuffle,
As we snicker and groan, dodging that shuffle.

You leave your shoes out, I step on the lace,
We share a long glance, then laugh at our race.
Partitioned in habits, we fight to adjust,
Yet in every mishap, there's love, there's trust.

Shared Air

We share the same air, yet dodge like we're shy,
Your pizza slice gone, oh my, oh my!
Between awkward silences, the laughter erupts,
Like two clowns in a circus, we're both just corrupt.

With morning routines, our chaos collides,
I steal your shampoo while you hide your fries.
In this comedy act, we stumble and sway,
Yet somehow we grin, come what may.

Melodies of Uncertainty

In rooms next door, music spills through the wall,
I hum your favorite song, but you don't call.
We play pretend, like twins from a show,
With sketches of lives that we both do not know.

Your cat finds my lap, like a soft little spy,
I swear he's plotting as he watches you sigh.
In this duet of quirks, we step on the beat,
Laughing at rhythms, oh what a treat!

The Distance of Breath

In the morning light, you snore like a bear,
I tiptoe around, giving you space and air.
The coffee pot brews as the clock loudly ticks,
We share this weird dance with all of its tricks.

The distance is funny, like shadows at dusk,
We tease and we bicker, but it's all just a must.
In this odd little home, we puzzle and play,
Creating our joys in the quirkiest way.

Echoes of Loneliness

In the kitchen, I hear a sigh,
The fridge hums like a sad lullaby.
A cat stalks the corners, tail held high,
She judges my toast with a critical eye.

With each bite, crumbs scatter like confetti,
The dog sneaks a piece; he thinks it's petty.
We laugh at the sound of a spoon that's unsteady,
Yet no one has seen me eating spaghetti.

The laundry spins tales of missing socks,
While I ponder why nobody knocks.
The couch often listens, it hears my knocks,
Yet here, it's just silence; we all fit in blocks.

One holds the remote, oh what a thrill,
While another recounts tales, it's never quite nil.
To chat with the walls is to climb a high hill,
Amidst all this quiet, we laugh and we chill.

Familiar Strangers

In the corner, the chair starts to creak,
Like it knows the secrets we dare not speak.
The rug has witnessed every little peak,
As we shuffle by, pretending to sneak.

I ask for a cookie; you roll your eyes,
"We just had dinner!" oh what a surprise!
Yet, I find one hidden, a sly little prize,
Familiarity breeds, but oh, the disguise.

The dishes pile high like a broken tower,
Yet somehow it feels like a sitcom hour.
We argue for fun, our favorite power,
While laughter over spills, it ends up a shower.

When hugs are a challenge, and words go awry,
We shuffle our feet, all shy and spry.
Under the surface, oh how we rely,
On familiar strangers, passing us by.

Hidden in Plain Sight

The sink is a fountain of secrets untold,
With dishes that cling like a thief in the fold.
I ponder my snacks, feeling bold,
Then trip on a toy, my balance sold.

A glimpse in the mirror, I see your face,
Contemplating soup with a curious grace.
We share a glance, it's our hidden place,
In a world full of laughter, we find our pace.

The TV blares out, a drama unfolds,
While we send sardonic texts, never too cold.
In this quaint little chaos, we break the mold,
Yet treasure the moments like glimmers of gold.

Last night's pizza box claims the throne,
While you haze a joke about it alone.
Echoes of laughter thrive and have grown,
In this space we share, a magic unknown.

A Thread Between

A pair of socks, mismatched just right,
Tugging my foot, they spark joy and fright.
We chuckle at how they squabble at night,
In the war of the laundry, a ridiculous sight.

I pour you coffee; you take it with flair,
But find sugar lumps scattered everywhere.
With laughter erupting; it lights up the air,
We take turns spilling secrets, blissfully rare.

The cat's got opinions on every last bite,
As we swap our stories, cozy delight.
In the silence that comes, it feels just right,
Connection, unbroken, ignites through the night.

So here we exist, in chaos and cheer,
In these tiny moments, we hold each dear.
A thread weaves us close, never sincere,
Yet laughter rings out, always loud and clear.

Walls of Silence

In the kitchen, pots collide,
While the cat yawns wide and bright.
Mom's on the phone with Aunt Louise,
Dad's lost his socks; it's quite a sight.

The dog chases ghosts on the floor,
We step over shoes, piled high.
Grandma tells tales from her chair,
But we nod, while our heads say goodbye.

An echo of laughter bounces back,
At dinner, nobody's on the same page.
We toast with our mugs, half-full of tea,
Yet someone forgot to turn off the sage.

In this circus, we're all quite close,
Yet miles apart in our minds.
We share the air, but with our quirks,
Our secret worlds we still find.

Homespun Distance

In the hall, my brother's loud,
While I try to read my book.
He thinks he's funny, I roll my eyes,
As he mimics the queen's funny look.

The TV blares a different tune,
Mom huffs while the laundry spins.
I'm hiding snacks in my room fast,
But Tim's on a search for wins.

Family dinners turn into debates,
Over who controls the TV time.
Sneaky snacks, a mission unspoken,
We each play our own little crime.

Laughter erupts like a full-blown storm,
Every joke, a comedic slide.
We stand together, yet drift apart,
In this dance, we still find pride.

Unspoken Spaces

My favorite chair is off-limits now,
That's where Dad dives for repose.
Meanwhile, Mom escalates the tea,
   Shushing the squabbling shows.

The vacuum roars, my sister screams,
   As I hide beneath the bed.
They don't hear me, just the machine,
   My laughter, like dust, gets spread.

At breakfast, silence fills the air,
Though we're gathered around the feast.
Jokes fly past, unwrapped like gifts,
   While cereal fights are the least.

In this weird home of invisible walls,
We play peek-a-boo with our hearts.
Every joke glimmers, bright yet vague,
Unspoken spaces, where laughter starts.

Ghosts in the Hallway

Shadows flit across the floor,
Echoes of steps we don't see.
Sister claims the couch is hers,
But I think it's haunting me.

Dinner table's a magic show,
With everyone pulling their puns.
Table manners? A distant ghost,
As we battle with forks and buns.

The plants have secrets, whispering soft,
While Dad talks to them like friends.
In our shared murmur, we thrive more,
On jokes that blossomed without ends.

Every corner hides a chuckle,
A specter of joy in our home.
We dance around our playful fights,
As friendly ghosts together roam.

Solitude in the Midst

In a house full of laughter, I'm all alone,
My snack thief sister swipes every scone.
Dad's snoring echoes like a loud, wild band,
While Mom's in the corner with her remote in hand.

They dance around me in a chaotic swirl,
I sneak a high-five with the invisible girl.
Cats plot their takeover, they own this space,
While I claim my throne, on the fridge, solace trace.

The sound of arguing fills the big room,
As I quietly hide, awaiting my doom.
My dog gives me looks with a raised, furry brow,
He knows all my secrets, oh boy, take a bow!

In this circus of home, I take a deep sigh,
And laugh at the chaos, while I quietly fly.
My mind makes a fortress, a cozy retreat,
Where people are loud, but my heart finds the beat.

The Weight of Unsaid Thoughts

At breakfast, we speak through the cereal crunch,
While Mom's slicing bread like she's planning a lunch.
Dad's deep in the news with a frown on his face,
And I'm imagining worlds where I go to space.

We nod and we smile, but we don't really chat,
Sharing a glance, but avoiding the spat.
Sister's up late with a mystery read,
While I zone out in a daydream, indeed.

The weight of the silence hangs thicker than fog,
As I ponder aloud if we're one big sitcom.
Laugh track plays softly when we trip or we fall,
But the truth is, we laugh at not laughing at all.

In this home of emotions left tangled and tight,
We giggle at shadows that haunt in the night.
Our hearts have a language, no sound finds its way,
In the weight of unsaid, we find laughter to play.

Comfort in Separate Shadows

In my own little corner, I plot and I scheme,
While family debates over who's lost the dream.
Sister's barking orders, while I build my fort,
My toys are my allies, in this secret court.

Mom's on the couch with her tea and her book,
While Dad stares at sports, it's the same old look.
Yet in my own world, I'm a king on a throne,
Where laughter's a whisper, but never alone.

Together yet distant, a puzzle we make,
As we tip-toe around for the sake of our break.
I'm hiding from chores, she's dodging the chat,
In the comfort of shadows, we're all just like that.

This space fills with chuckles, yet keeps us apart,
In the realm of our silence, we share every heart.
In the dance of the mundane, we secretly bask,
Finding joy in our laughter, unmasked with a mask.

Love That Drifts

In our home of quirks, love drifts like a breeze,
While Dad cracks a joke, and everyone flees.
Mom rolls her eyes, but oh, it's so sweet,
As chaos unfolds on this family street.

Sister's on her phone, in a bubble of clouds,
I'm lost in the fridge, making food for the crowds.
Together we giggle, yet float like balloons,
Our spirits all lifted, like a grand afternoon.

Each step in this dance is a step out of sync,
Yet we twirl through the kitchen, like stars on the brink.
With love that just drifts, it's unpredictable cheer,
Our laughter flows freely, no burden or fear.

So while we may wander in our separate ways,
The heart of this home is a wild, joyful maze.
In this jumbled-up world, we find quite the spark,
Love that drifts and dances, lighting up the dark.

The Silence in Our Love

In a room so close, yet far away,
Your socks are loud, my silence stays.
We dance around, avoiding a fight,
Your breakfast crumbs are a comical sight.

I talk to walls, they never reply,
You smile at screens, like they're nearby.
Love's a puzzle, pieces misplaced,
Yet we both wear our grumpy face.

A humor found in every glance,
Like strangers forced to share a dance.
The cat's our kid, so wise and sly,
He knows we're laughing, oh my, oh my!

So here we are, a funny pair,
In our own world, without a care.
With every chuckle, life's a jest,
In this awkward love, we're truly blessed.

Divergent Hearts Under the Same Sky

You like it cold, I crank up heat,
Our thermostat's a battle we greet.
Your coffee's black, mine's sweet as pie,
We're a mismatched team, oh me, oh my!

We watch the show, you groan and boo,
I laugh so hard, what's wrong with you?
Our tastes collide in comedic ways,
Two divergent souls in funny plays.

I hide the snacks, you hunt around,
Stealthy as ninjas, make not a sound.
With every laugh, the world's anew,
In our odd dance, it's just us two.

We are two as one, it's quite absurd,
You snore a tune, and I'm disturbed.
Yet in this chaos, so clear, so bright,
Together apart, we hold on tight.

The Lonely Symphony of Us

In the living room, your hum goes flat,
I join in loud with a silly spat.
Our mismatched symphony fills the air,
Like cats in chorus, it's a funny affair.

You strum the chords, I play the mime,
Our tunes entwined, yet we miss the rhyme.
With forks as microphones, we belt our song,
A duet of laughter that feels so wrong.

The dog joins in, he barks the beat,
As our concert thrives on a cushion seat.
We dance with glee, both side by side,
In this comical chaos, we will abide.

So here we stand, an orchestra strange,
Sweet dissonance, it's funny, not vain.
In our lonely concert, we'll shine like stars,
Creating a love that's truly ours.

Togetherness with an Asterisk

We share the space but not the bed,
You hog the sheets, I'm left for dead.
Your midnight snacks, they call my name,
Yet you pretend I'm not your game.

Our laughter bursts like popcorn, bright,
You steal the covers, but it feels so right.
The "us" that's more than just a fact,
An asterisk hints at the love we act.

With every day, our quirks collide,
Like playful rivals, where we both slide.
We bicker loudly, and then we sigh,
But the love we share can't be denied.

So here's to us, the oddest blend,
With foot rubs and pouts, we always mend.
Together, apart, it's hilariously true,
In the fun of it all, I still choose you.

Distant Touches

We're sharing a couch, but on different screens,
You're lost in a meme, I'm critiquing cuisine.
Your socks are a mystery, mine smell like cheese,
Yet somehow we laugh, and the tension does ease.

In the kitchen, I dance; you ignore my moves,
I offer you snacks, but you've got other grooves.
The dishes pile up, like a tower of pride,
Yet I know you'll still smile when you step to my side.

At night we both snooze, but in separate beds,
You comfort your pillow, I dream of bread spreads.
The dog likes you better; he snorts by your feet,
While I steal the blanket, how unfair is this feat?

Yet somehow in chaos, a bond remains clear,
Two clashing rhythms that somehow endear.
Our lives like a sitcom, both funny and real,
In this circus of distance, we dance with great zeal.

Ghosts of Each Other's Presence

You haunt the living room, a beautiful ghost,
Your laughter a memory that I cherish most.
I swear I just heard you, like a soft gentle breeze,
It turns out it's just my imagination that teases.

Your shoes by the door look like they're still there,
Yet when I go searching, it's just empty air.
The fridge hums your tune, it echoes your face,
We're living in echoes, yet I crave your embrace.

You left your old shirt, it calls out my name,
Each wrinkle a story, but it's not quite the same.
I talk to the shadows, they nod in accord,
But it's your silly jokes that I always adored.

At times I just giggle at our silly ballet,
Two spirits entwined in a clumsy display.
Though distance defines us, this laughter won't cease,
Our playful hauntings bring a strange kind of peace.

Lives Untangled Yet Close

In our shared chaos, we're tangled for sure,
You hog all the snacks while I'm left with a cure.
Your socks are a maze of unmatched delight,
Yet somehow these quirks make our days feel just right.

With calendars crossed out in colors so bright,
We plan our adventures, but things go awry.
You're off to the store, while I binge watch the show,
When you're back, my snacks are a sweet overflow.

We're like puzzle pieces that don't quite align,
Yet somehow we fit in this silly design.
Your late-night whispers, the popcorn you steal,
Makes life much more fun; it's a quirky appeal.

So here's to our stories, the laughs we ignite,
Lives intertwined, yet both taking flight.
In our clashing rhythms, a sweet harmony plays,
We're crafting a symphony in zany array.

The Uninvited Space

There's this quiet bubble that's filled up with air,
It floats in the corner, does anyone care?
I vacuum each corner, but dust bunnies thrive,
With laughter and chaos, they help us survive.

Your laundry's a fortress, it's quite the large maze,
I tiptoe around it in a comical phase.
You throw in a comment, I toss back a quip,
And in this odd standoff, we share every trip.

The dog thinks he's king, on a throne made of snacks,
We feign at compliance while planning our tracks.
There's space on the couch, but you're crowding my feet,
Yet somehow your weirdness makes everything sweet.

So here's to the distance, this playful charade,
A tug-of-war laughter, where memories fade.
In the uninvited, we craft a delight,
Our silly adventures are pure dynamite!

Shadows in the Shared Space

In the kitchen, you brew your tea,
While I'm plotting my victory spree.
You dance with dishes, a clumsy waltz,
And I trip on shoes, it's all your faults.

Your socks strewn wide, the couch is a mess,
I made a fortress; it's all just excess.
We share the fridge, but not the crust,
Avoiding each other, it's a must!

Laughter leaks through thin walls at night,
Tales of our battles, a comical fight.
You scream at the TV, I roll my eyes,
But when you laugh, it's the best surprise!

We vacuum and dodge, sharing the room,
Playing hide and seek in the morning gloom.
Your shadow creeps, while I hide my grin,
Together in chaos, but where to begin?

Heartbeats Divided by Walls

My heart beats solo, yours thumps a tune,
In separate rooms we commune with the moon.
You hoard the snacks while I stash the cheese,
We tiptoe 'round like it's an escape tease.

Your playlist blares, I grin in defeat,
Yet dance on tiptoes, avoid your beat.
Each heartbeat echoes in this zany maze,
A rhythm of chaos through the night's haze.

You cook with sass, I bake with flair,
Flour on your face, but you don't care.
We share recipes, with a pinch of spite,
Two chefs in a kitchen, yet not quite right.

Our bickering's loud, but so is the fun,
Like a clown and a jester, we've barely won.
With heartbeats dancing, but apart we stay,
In this circus of life, we both have our say!

Silence Between the Rooms

In the hallway, silence reigns supreme,
Except for your humming, what a sweet dream!
I tiptoe past, avoiding your stares,
Like a ninja in stealth, it's full of flares.

You whisk with glee, and I lounge like a cat,
Catching snippets of your soft chit-chat.
We could share silence, but why would we dare?
Instead, it's a race, who'll break the air?

There's grace in this mess, a comedy plot,
Every small noise just entangles the knot.
You fumble the keys and I spill my drink,
In this shared quiet, we both rethink.

Yet somehow we laugh, as we dodge and engage,
In this funny play, we're stuck on the stage.
Two hearts in alignment, though silence may loom,
With laughs at the edges, we lighten the gloom!

Together Yet Alone

In this space, together we stay,
While our jokes melt like butter away.
Your snoring's a symphony, all through the night,
Yet in the morning, we both feel just right.

You hog all the blankets, I shiver and pout,
Accusing you slyly, but we laugh it out.
Two worlds collide in snickers and sneers,
Making sweet chaos out of mundane years.

Your side of the bed is a fortress of dreams,
While I'm lost in thoughts, or so it seems.
Together yet tangled, we're quirky, it's true,
A blend of our quirks, an odd living view.

So here's to the laughter, the fun and the fights,
In this daft little love, we spark up the nights.
Together we bumble, through life's funny show,
Two jesters in tandem, oh what a glow!

Lingering Absences

You dance in the kitchen, I roast in the sun,
Our greetings are parties, but no one has won.
You laugh at the jokes that I never can tell,
In parallel laughter, we're both under a spell.

The laundry's a mountain, socks missing their mates,
You claim that the fridge is an ancient temple of plates.
We share all our snacks, though you eat them all whole,
As you giggle alone, I'm there in my bowl.

Our cat takes your side, it's a well-planned coup,
She pretends I'm invisible, like I'm out of the view.
You sip on your tea, with a smirk and a shrug,
While I'm wrestling with chores like a reluctant bug.

So here we stand, both in our separate spheres,
With love so stretched out, it's beyond mortal years.
In moments we're close, yet so distant in space,
Who knew being apart could be such a fun race?

The Comfort of Distance

You're a wizard of snacks, a wizard of sound,
While I'm cloaked in my silence, you dance all around.
I pen all my letters to walls made of wood,
You snicker at whispers, but it's understood.

We trade funny glances across the big room,
A game of charades, like a cartoonish zoom.
Your pets seem to chuckle at my half-hearted sighs,
They're judging my logic with those wise, furry eyes.

You're never around when the laundry needs folding,
Yet you find all my secrets that I keep from unfolding.
We both love the laughter, the bickering too,
It's love in odd corners, like a whimsical zoo.

In mismatched communion, we thrive day by day,
Distance is cozy, just look at how we play!
With antics and pranks, we enjoy this great art,
Ever close at the edges, but miles from the heart.

Disjointed Harmony

Our rhythms are tangled, a curious beat,
You love the loud music, while I hide away, discreet.
Your jokes are like fireworks, bursting and bright,
While I'm a whisper, a shadow in twilight.

You hum in the kitchen, while I'm stuck in my chair,
Your laughter's a symphony, a wild flair.
I fumble with words, you're a comedian's dream,
We play out our roles, the absurd, silly team.

Your side of the bed is a loveable mess,
While I keep my space tidy, I must confess.
You steal all the sunshine, I harbor the shade,
In a duet of chaos, our song's never frayed.

We're mismatched like socks, yet a fanciful pair,
Creating a comedy, a joy we can share.
In this ludicrous life, together we roam,
With laughter as glue, we're building our home.

In the Same Space

We're two ships in a harbor, but sailing apart,
Your compass goes north, mine's stuck in a chart.
You rattle the dishes while I quietly scheme,
A circus of chaos, you're the main of my dream.

In the land of mismatching, we stumble and trip,
Your trips around corners are a comical script.
You joke about socks that have vanished from sight,
While I'm drowning in blankets with a pillow fight.

The schedule's a puzzle, your plans have no end,
You offer big parties, I send them to blend.
You make me a sandwich with twice the wrong spread,
But we laugh 'til we cry, that's the joy that we've bred.

In quirky companionship, we're thriving just fine,
Two jesters in life, or a mismatched design.
As we weave our own stories, let the fun never stop,
In this whimsical journey, together we'll hop.

Aching Silence Amidst Laughter

In the room, a joke is told,
Yet you sit, a grin, not bold.
A sneeze, a cough, the laughter fades,
The silence wraps like silly shades.

A dance-off starts, you tap your feet,
But watch the chaos from your seat.
They laugh, they twirl, the floor's a mess,
While you just sip your soda, yes!

The dog's in charge, it takes a leap,
As silent giggles start to creep.
You're "enjoying" every scene,
Still deeply lost in comfy dreams.

A plate of snacks, a burst of cheer,
You muffle snickers, hold your beer.
Amid the fun, you sip alone,
While laughter echoes off the phone.

Shifting Shadows in Light

The walls are bright, the shadows sway,
While you pretend to work and play.
Your friend's a mime, a silent jest,
You snicker loud, ignore the rest.

A game of charades, a pose so grand,
You twist your face, they can't understand.
You're in the game but still just chill,
Behind the scenes, you've found your thrill.

A mock debate on who's the best,
You vote for snacks—no time for rest.
The laughter swells, your smile shines,
Yet all the fun's from distant lines.

The hour creeps, the fun's a race,
But you just smile, not in the chase.
In this bright room, you sip your drink,
While shadows dance and strangers wink.

Whispering Walls

The walls converse with little sighs,
As silly tales fly through the skies.
You smirk alone, a quiet knight,
While laughter bursts, the room's alight.

A high-five echoes, but you just stare,
At all the chaos, at all the flair.
A cup spills wine, a laugh erupts,
Your heart races, while silence cups.

The jokes they tell, you've heard them all,
You chuckle soft from your cozy hall.
While inside jokes weave through the air,
You raise your glass with a cheeky flair.

Like shadows whispering through the night,
You smile along, but not quite right.
Amid the fun, you hold the reins,
In this silly, sweet refrain.

Echoes of Distance

The party hums like busy bees,
While you enjoy your little tease.
A toast rings out, then laughter swells,
You sip your drink—fishing for shells.

With every jest, you share a glance,
Yet dance alone in this quirky trance.
A trivia game, you know the score,
But cheer from far; you won't implore.

Eyes roll, you laugh at every jest,
But from a corner, you feel blessed.
The echoes bounce from wall to wall,
While you just sit and soak it all.

When jokes collide like funny fate,
You play the quiet, cool escape.
In this raucous symphony of cheer,
You're near but far—your smile sincere.

Soft Feet on Hard Floors

In the kitchen, I sneak and glide,
Hoping to avoid the creaky side.
The cat just watched with narrowed eyes,
As I tiptoe past, a clumsy disguise.

My cereal's loud, it crunches away,
While my roommate snores, dreaming astray.
They'll never know it's me out of bed,
As I dance with shadows, a breakfast ballet.

But who needs silence in the morning light?
A clatter of spoons, a giggle in flight.
We share this space yet play our roles,
Two silent performers with mismatched goals.

So here's to the floors, both hard and sleek,
And the soft little beep of my phone's quirky tweak.
Together but slightly out of sync,
Sharing this house, with no time to think.

Separate Dreams in Shared Nights

While you dream of castles with dragons so grand,
I'm wrestling monsters with popcorn in hand.
Your snores like thunder, mine hiccups of glee,
A symphony of slumber, oh what a spree!

We share the blanket, a tug-of-war game,
You steal all the room, but I'll still take the blame.
Moonlight spills secrets through curtains so frilly,
As I laugh at your dreams, which are often quite silly.

Our pillows like barriers, but friendly disputes,
Dreams wrapped in laughter, like mismatched suits.
Two worlds collide, yet stay so apart,
In this sleepy haven, bright joy fills the heart.

So, here's to the night, with its whimsical sights,
Two dreamers collide in their quirky delights.
One's lost in fantasy, the other in puns,
Under the stars, no need for runs.

Floating in Familiar Skies

On lazy Sundays, we float and we roam,
Each in our bubble, our heavenly dome.
Your favorite show, my comic strip spree,
Two separate worlds, but still full of glee.

You with your coffee, and I with my tea,
Juggling our screens, like a mad symphony.
We could be sailing on clouds made of fluff,
But let's stay grounded, it's more than enough.

We glance up and smile, from time to time,
A wink through the chaos, a moment in rhyme.
Though sharing the space, we're on different flights,
With laughter as fuel, we scale the heights.

Navigating close, yet so far away,
In this cozy air, we unwind and play.
With inside jokes that make no sense to most,
Floating together, we're a whimsical boast.

The Heart's Invisible Distance

In the living room, we're worlds apart,
You scroll through feeds while I doodle art.
We wave a hello, but our eyes stay keen,
Two ships passing by, in our cozy marine.

You're lost in your thoughts, I'm tangled in mine,
Cracks in the silence like notes on a line.
Yet laughter erupts, like popcorns we pop,
Caught in the moment, we're never a flop.

The fridge hums a tune, a familiar sound,
While my shoes scatter chaos, they've never been found.
We share a heartbeat yet drive each other mad,
In this lovely odd dance, both happy and glad.

So here's to the distance we bridge every day,
With humor and kindness, in our quirky ballet.
We navigate space, both near and far,
In this wild adventure, we're each other's star.

A Tapestry of Lonely Threads

In the kitchen, we dance, but avoid the same step,
Your coffee's too strong, like a wild, raucous pet.
I hide in my room with snacks piled high,
While you binge on shows, our laughter awry.

A sock on the floor, it's our silent parade,
Waging a war, neither side is afraid.
Your face in the fridge, my shadow in sight,
We'll meet at the dinner, but just for a bite.

The couch is a fortress, we're kings of our space,
With snacks for our subjects, no need to embrace.
I'll cheer for my team while you cheer for the cat,
A raucous alliance, like soldiers all flat.

So here's to the chaos of love and of fun,
In a house where together is never quite done.
With quirky connections in quirky routines,
We thrive in this dance of our silly scenes.

The Unvoiced Connection

In the hallway, your shoes are a clue of your day,
But my wit's on the shelf, in a comical way.
You'll snicker at nothing; I'll chuckle at sprawl,
While we keep our banter, but never in thrall.

You send me a meme that I roll my eyes at,
I respond with a shrug, just a polite spat.
We share the same fridge, a unison plight,
But my cake is a treasure, yours, just a bite.

The bathroom's a groundhog day circle of dread,
I hear you in there, sighing gently, misled.
Yet under our glares, there's a playful duet,
Of eyes that say 'hi' without cashing the check.

So to love in the silence and jokes never told,
In the warmth of the shared space, our hearts uncontrolled.

We may be apart in our glorious sprout,
But the laughter we weave is what life's all about.

Cohabiting Yet Apart

You claim the living room, it's your kingdom, it's true,
While I plot in the kitchen with my trusty fondue.
The vacuum is royal, your throne on a chair,
Yet the dust bunnies giggle, a curious affair.

Across the wide room, our eyes often meet,
Over cereal barriers, we dodge and repeat.
A sneeze breaks the silence, we cautiously grin,
In this wacky abode, where the fun might begin.

You sing in the shower, I strum on my couch,
Together creating a sound like a slouch.
The laundry piles high, a colorful mound,
We laugh at this tangle, not a care in the round.

So cheers to the chaos where we sit far apart,
With a wink and a laugh, there's a warmth in the heart.
Through quips and through quirks, we'll always survive,
In this quirky cocoon, where the fun's kept alive.

Parallel Heartbeats

You grab the remote, I seize the last slice,
A battle of wills, oh how we think twice.
Your memes crack a smile, my puns earn a sigh,
But shadows of laughter can't ever run dry.

We share narrow hallways with poetic grunts,
And scenes become breezy as our humor confronts.
I hide sweets in drawers, while you claim the couch,
But it's a fond rivalry, not an outright slouch.

Through doors that remain ever slightly ajar,
Life's quirks twinkle brightly like a distant star.
Our schedules collide in a rhythm, a dance,
With unspoken jokes and a whimsical chance.

So here's to the moments of happy affection,
In a waltz built of snickers, a cozy connection.
You may watch your own show, I'll revel in mine,
Yet side by side, we make an odd kind of shine.

Rooms with Unfulfilled Dreams

In my cozy nook, I ponder,
Why the snacks keep disappearing!
My fridge holds secrets so much fonder,
Yet my diet woes still keep me drearing.

My cat plots schemes, I swear she's wise,
Stealing my socks and my last slice!
We're roommates here, without disguise,
I'll draft a treaty, that sounds nice.

The vacuum roars, it knows my fears,
For it's a ghost in my daily grind!
Cleaning up crumbs, not shedding tears,
At least the dust bunnies are quite kind.

Oh, to share a laugh through the wall,
When I trip over shoes left unclaimed!
Each stumble earns me a laughter call,
In this odd dance, it's never the same!

Togetherness in Isolation

I'm on a zoom call, but who's behind?
My neighbor's dog just took the stage!
His bark must surely be one of a kind,
Can't blame him; it's tough to engage!

While I sip my coffee, cold and gray,
My kid is conducting a symphony loud.
Through laughter and chaos, we'll find a way,
In the living room, the circus is proud.

Text messages fly like friendly darts,
Inviting to gather, yet there we stay.
With screens as our windows, we play our parts,
Recreating friendship from far away.

But if we tried to meet face-to-face,
We'd just end up at the fridge, it's true!
Still cozy here, in our little space,
Craving human touch, and snacks too!

Fragmented Familiarity

In the hallway, we nod and smile,
Yet the distance feels like a mile.
I know your snacks but not your name,
This quirky dance is a fun little game.

Each day an opera, our lives collide,
The clash of laundry is our silly pride.
Whispers travel through the thin wall,
Could it be gossip? Or just a call?

We share the Wi-Fi, but not the couch,
I watch your show, you binge on mine!
A soap opera plot where we lovingly slouch,
Yet it feels too right, this quirky design.

On weekends, I hear your TV's cheer,
While my plants plot revenge—they stare!
Together yet apart, year after year,
Who knew these quirks could be our affair?

Hidden Longings in Shared Spaces

We share a roof, yet rooms are divided,
The popcorn stalls in the cine-mood!
You're in your bubble, I've decided,
To find solitude, but oh, I'm gooed!

A pot of tea brews with a secret scheme,
While you laugh loudly at your own loud past.
Two worlds collide in a whimsical dream,
Together in silence, but never too fast.

Our front door opens with a cheerful ding,
As packages come with hopes and glee.
But peeking through, I won't take a fling,
I'll keep this distance; it's quite the spree.

Let's toast with mugs from our separate nooks,
Remote friendship with joy, we persist!
In this strange setup, we'll write our books,
Laughter trailing in hallways, we'll coexist!

Within Reach

Two rooms, one house, what a twist,
We both chuckle at what we've missed.
You cook pasta, I burn the bread,
Our little battles fought without dread.

The laundry piles up, who's to blame?
We play the blame game, it's all the same.
You steal my socks, I take your book,
Inthis comedy, we give each other a look.

Shopping lists, they're not the same,
Your 'essentials' make me shift in shame.
Half a bag of chips, a forgotten snack,
We joke about our pantry's lack.

Late-night giggles, muffled and real,
We share secrets, over a meal.
Who needs boundaries when we can jest?
In our quirky home, we're truly blessed.

Beyond Touch

You're in your zone, I'm in mine,
A dance of distance, it's divine.
Netflix marathons, we watch apart,
Our laughs collide, but don't quite start.

You're in your chair with a cup of joe,
While I'm racing through my own little show.
A playful war of volume and cheer,
We make our way, yet keep it clear.

Sometimes I wonder, is this for fun?
Trading our stories, still on the run.
You say pizza, I crave ice cream,
In this distance, we still team.

Odd little rituals, our stubborn ways,
Making memories through the haze.
Together we thrive, yet drift in stride,
Through all our chaos, we take pride.

Muffled Conversations

Walls do not block our silly chats,
Just a door separates our spats.
You laugh at my puns, they're such a treat,
I roll my eyes—you're my favorite cheat.

Echoes of joy filter through the night,
A pillow fort waiting to feel just right.
Your side is quiet, mine's a parade,
We joke that 'serious' might just fade.

Rattling dishes with gleeful sound,
Chopsticks are flinging, let's gather 'round.
Muffled debates over who's the best,
All's well when laughter beats the rest.

In our bubble of snickers and quirks,
We find our joy, where silliness lurks.
Separate spaces, but hearts entwined,
In our cozy chaos, love's redefined.

Whispers in the Hallway

Sneaking snacks in our little lane,
Shh! Don't wake the sleepy bane.
You tiptoe past, I hold my breath,
Your love for cookies merits a theft.

We share the hall with stolen sighs,
A glimpse of mischief in our eyes.
You plot revenge for a sugar spree,
My quiet chuckles, your secret glee.

Sneaky notes stuck to the wall,
'You're the best!'—not a hint of brawl.
But just last week, you held my mug,
And I retaliated with a playful shrug.

In whispers soft, our tales abound,
A mischief maker, I'm shorter ground.
Together we roam, a funny crew,
These whispered moments, me and you.

Parallel Lives in Close Quarters

Your cereal's sweet, mine's distinct,
Two taste buds dance, making us linked.
In the morning bustle, we're side by side,
With playful jabs and smiles wide.

While you jog, I skip in place,
We both get fit, but at our own pace.
Who won the race? Who really knows?
Just two competitors in all our woes.

You prefer books, I claim the screen,
In our living room, we've both seen,
A comedy where quirks collide,
In mismatched pairings, we take pride.

Through laughter and chaos, side by side,
We navigate life, with joy as our guide.
Together apart, we flourish and glow,
In this funny little show, we steal the show.

Shared Shadows

In the fridge, that last slice waits,
Mama claims it's hers, she debates.
But little Timmy's sneaky plan,
A heist with grip, a stealthy man.

As laundry mounts, the socks all flee,
One socks says, "Why don't we agree?"
To form a club, escape the wash,
And find a life that's truly posh.

At movie night, they take their space,
Mom's popcorn mounds, a fluffy grace.
Yet dad's remote, his secret prize,
Is wielded like a sword to rise.

Laughter echoes, chases start,
They share a home, but need their part.
With jokes and pranks, it's quite the show,
In this crazy house, the love just flows.

Silent Echoes

Dishes piled, a mountain tall,
Dad sneezes, and they all will fall.
Mom whispers softly, "Not my chore,"
While dishes dance, they all want more.

The dog, he knows to fetch the mail,
He plays the part, he won't go stale.
But every time, it's not the task,
It's treats he seeks, no need to ask.

Each room a realm, a different zone,
Where silence reigns, and laughs are grown.
The toilet seat, a common fight,
But jokes ensue in the dead of night.

Silent battles, but joy we weave,
In tangled threads, so hard to cleave.
Cups clink softly, a toast to fate,
In quirky ways, we celebrate.

Fractured Togetherness

Three TVs blare in perfect sync,
Each lost in worlds, no time to think.
Dad yells, "This is the best scene!"
While others roll their eyes, unseen.

Dinner's served, one's vegan, one's not,
"Pass the broccoli!"not a thought.
But laughter spills from mismatched plates,
Where love still grows despite the fates.

A sibling war, a pillow fight,
Mom tosses snacks, not quite polite.
Yet giggles clash in soft delight,
In fractured joy, they shine so bright.

Though paths diverge within this space,
Each one finds their special place.
With playful slams and sweet retorts,
They bond in laughter, no last resorts.

Parallel Lives

Every morning, coffee brews,
Yet flavors clash, they all choose blues.
One takes sweet, another salt,
In this war of taste, no one's at fault.

The cat claims territory with pride,
While clueless dog just wags and hides.
One can't stop barking up a tree,
While whiffs from tuna set the cat free.

Homework battles, the crayons fly,
"Don't touch my stuff!" they moan and sigh.
But collaged dreams come to unite,
In messy rooms, creativity's might.

With chores assigned, they wrangle on,
Just making sure, no task is gone.
Through raucous giggles, they learn to thrive,
In this big chaos, they're truly alive.

The Threads That Bind Yet Separate

We're all here at home, tucked in tight,
But my socks disappear, a daring flight.
You hide in your room, like it's a game,
While I wear your shirt, it's pretty lame.

We share the fridge, yet I can't find,
The last slice of pizza, you're one of a kind.
We pass in the hall, it's like a race,
Avoiding eye contact, what a strange space.

The TV blares loudly, but I'm not there,
Lost in my thoughts, looking for air.
Your laugh echoes through walls, so near,
Yet I'd trade it for quiet, just for a year.

In this home of ours, we laugh and we groan,
Too close for comfort, but still all alone.
The threads that we're weaving pull tight and twist,
Better live with the chaos, it's hard to resist.

Layers of Unnoticed Solitude

In corners we linger, like shadows cast,
Sharing this space, but not seeing the past.
Your cereal crunches, it breaks the calm,
While I'm pondering life, oh what a charm.

Layers of silence, thicker than pie,
You're right in the next room, but I still sigh.
We laugh through our screens, in an uncanny way,
Yet feel like we're oceans and drifting away.

Dinner is served, but we're lost in our phones,
Each bite is a battle, we're far from our homes.
There's joy in the mundane, or so I'm told,
Yet I wish for connection, but the silence is bold.

Together in spirit, but miles in our heads,
Funny how comfort can feel like it spreads.
Cracking a joke, but it falls on deaf ears,
Laughing together, yet shedding no tears.

Conversations with No Words

We sit at breakfast, no words to share,
You pour your coffee, I pretend to care.
The rustle of paper, a sigh in the air,
For all the talk, there's nothing that's fair.

Your glance says 'fine', while I just nod,
In a world of chatter, it feels a bit odd.
The laughter we fake, is it all for show?
Invisible strings pull, where did they go?

We dance around topics, like cats on a floor,
Ducking and weaving, is there something in store?
A quip here or there, but nobody bites,
Conversations of silence, oh what a plight.

Days blur together, it's funny, you see,
How we're always close, yet lost as can be.
With smiles like band-aids on our lonely hearts,
Is it friendship or just where the awkwardness starts?

Emptiness Amidst the Clamor

The music is loud, but my heart feels small,
With voices like thunder that echo the hall.
We toast and we cheer, but I miss the tease,
A nod from the sofa, just off by degrees.

You're dancing around, all rhythm and glee,
But still, as I watch, it's a one-man spree.
The laughter rings out, bouncing off walls,
Yet in the cacophony, solitude calls.

We yell through the noise, hoping we're heard,
But nobody knows what we mean by our word.
The emptiness lingers, a bittersweet blob,
In the party of life, we're just part of the mob.

When the clamor subsides, we glance sideways,
It's funny how families can drift in their ways.
Together yet distant, a comic charade,
In the silence that follows, the echoes don't fade.

Separate Paths Beneath One Sky

In the kitchen, a brawl ensues,
Spaghetti flies, we've all got the blues.
'It's your fault!' I yell with a grin,
As sauce stains my shirt, where to begin?

On the couch, you claim the whole seat,
While I wrestle the dog for my feet.
We both laugh at the dog's sly retreat,
Our sitcom lives, far from discreet.

You fetch the remote, but with a twist,
In our own little worlds, we persist.
Shared jokes floating in the air we flout,
But still pretend we're alone, no doubt.

Yet in these battles of laugh and play,
We are woven in our unique way.
Each war over snacks, a quirky fight,
Together alone, we're quite the sight!

Fractured Togetherness

You take the left side, I guard the right,
In the chaos we call our daily life.
The laundry's piled high, a mountain of dread,
Yet socks disappear – where's that one red?

We argue who's turn it is to clean,
While binge-watching snacks in our messy scene.
The dishes stack up like a teetering tower,
But our laughter erupts, a bonding power.

On mismatched chairs, we gather to eat,
Cheese in the fridge, a smelly treat.
Your bites are gleeful, mine are a wreck,
Yet pie means truce, what the heck!?

The remote is lost, but we just don't care,
Silly debates spark joy in the air.
We step on each other's toes all the time,
But in this comedy, life's truly a rhyme!

Unshared Memories Adrift

In the attic lies our box of dreams,
Full of memories, or so it seems.
You're rummaging through, while I just snooze,
'Did we have fun, or just lose our shoes?'

The photos we take always end with a laugh,
Except that one time with the goat on the path.
Your face turned red, mine from the mud,
Together we giggle, lost in the flood.

You crafted a story, I made a mess,
Our tales of woe, aren't they the best?
Your childhood dreams of dancing bears,
While I'm stuck knowing you still hate stairs.

We drink our tea, but I spill the brew,
While you chuckle, it's nothing new.
In this quirky world, we sail our ships,
Two different seas, yet we share the slips!

Solitary Corners of Togetherness

In the corner lies your clownish grin,
While I huddle where the quiet begins.
You play the fool with jokes on repeat,
While I plan my escape from this seat.

The fridge is stocked with weird things to eat,
Each leftover's a mystery—spicy or sweet?
You giggle as I take a brave chance,
But my face reveals a curious dance.

You dance in the hallway, arms flailing wide,
While I navigate obstacles, hoping to hide.
You can't hear my laughter, it's trapped in my chest,
Both separated by our very own best.

In these quirky circles of our odd little life,
With laughter and chaos, and maybe some strife.
Here's to the silly, the fun we create,
Together we thrive, while apart in our fate!

The Distance in Our Embrace

We share the fridge, but not the snacks,
You raid my stash—I plot my attacks.
A dance in the kitchen, feet all a-tangle,
Yet someone's forgotten to clean up the bangle.

Your jokes fall flat, my laughs are snorts,
Trading puns like playful retorts.
You say I'm crazy, I call you weird,
In this quirky circus, we're both quite steered.

The laundry's a battle, socks in disarray,
The cat's my therapist; she hears what I say.
But when you're not home, it's just too quiet,
I'd trade the silence for our playful riot.

So here's to this life, with quirks and delight,
Two peas in a pod, but still out of sight.
With humor our glue, we'll weather the storm,
In this crazy world, you keep me warm.

Echoes of Unspoken Words

I talk to the walls, they nod in reply,
When you're on the couch, we can't make eye.
I swear you hide when chores come around,
Yet here I find breadcrumbs—a magic profound.

You keep the remote like it's your best friend,
While I scheme and plot for the TV to bend.
A glance at the clock, oh look, it's quite late,
But the snacks on the table have sealed our fate.

Mornings are quiet, no words need to flow,
Picking up coffee amidst all the show.
Your shirt's on my chair, my shoes are in yours,
How did we plan such completely mixed chores?

So let silence reign with laughter so near,
We dance in our chaos and let out a cheer.
Two souls in the zone, yet worlds apart,
In this home of ours—an odd work of art.

A House Full of Solitude

The bathroom's busy, it's all locked tight,
While I shout through the door, "Just one more night!"
You hum in the shower, I roll my eyes,
Trading our space for privacy lies.

The living room's mine, a fortress of snacks,
Your Netflix account? I leave it with hacks.
Doodles on napkins, our thoughts set free,
A shared sense of humor, just you wait and see.

Dinner's a circus, a plate juggled high,
We laugh as our pasta takes quite a fly.
Though chaos reigns, there's love in the fight,
In this house of solitude, we feel just right.

With walls unseen, yet laughter so loud,
We thrive in the mess, and oh, we're so proud!
Two hearts intertwined, with quirks so divine,
In this grand theater, you'll always be mine.

The Unseen Divide

You claim the corner, I hug the wall,
Yet the couch is the territory for all.
In our kingdom of chaos, we play hide and seek,
With pillows as shields, it's an epic peak.

When you're on the phone, it's a secret debate,
I swear I'm not listening; let's not seal our fate.
We giggle at puns that are cringeworthy bad,
But in this odd dance, who would ever be sad?

I tripped on your shoes, now you owe me a snack,
You find it quite funny, while I check my back.
Our laughter is music, a glitch in the plan,
Two individuals dancing—oh yes, that's the jam!

At the end of the day, as the lights dim down,
We share inside jokes—nobody wears a frown.
In our little haven, both alone and together,
We thrive on the jest; our hearts are forever.

Individual Journeys Side by Side

In a house that sways and creaks,
My coffee's strong while his tea leaks.
Laundry piles up, a mountain high,
Yet here we stand, a sister and guy.

We share the fridge, but not the snack,
He claims the couch—I'm planning my attack.
Half the time we text from our rooms,
Laughing at memes through Wi-Fi fumes.

Dinner's a race, who'll get there first?
I grab the spoon; he grabs dessert.
We argue loud, then burst in cheer,
While sharing space but not quite near.

In these whimsical walls, life can be grand,
Just don't touch my stuff, or I won't understand.
Two separate paths, yet we collide,
In our quirky dance, we find our stride.

Uncarved Connections

You steal the blankets every night,
While I battle shadows, giving you a fright.
Echoes of laughter and occasional sighs,
Two souls adrift, with mismatched ties.

Your socks on the floor, my shoes in a heap,
We complicate order, but in chaos we leap.
A shared Wi-Fi password, the ultimate bond,
Yet at the same time, we're both so fond.

Kitchen experiments, we both partake,
Some meals delicious, others a mistake.
You stole my fries, it was quite a heist,
Yet I'll laugh it off, and share your slice.

In this fine mess, we find our way,
With stories of life shared over the day.
Together yet separate in this cozy space,
A dance of confusion, with smiles on our face.

Constant Proximity

In our little bubble, the world spins wide,
Your sass is the wave; I'm just on the tide.
Side-by-side, yet miles apart,
In whispered jokes, we make our art.

You blare your tunes, it drives me insane,
But I fake a dance-off, trying to feign.
In this wild rhythm, we lose the beat,
And laugh at the chaos, oh so sweet.

The clock strikes eleven, you crave a late bite,
But I'm zonked out, dreaming of flight.
With snacks in hand, you tiptoe around,
We're in constant proximity, in silence profound.

In this mixed-up world, we share a glance,
Laughter erupts in our odd little dance.
Forever together, yet free to roam,
In our friendly fortress, we've made a home.

Fleeting Touch

The couch feels crowded—why's your foot there?
I nudge you gently, but you just stare.
A bump of elbows, the fight for room,
In our awkward waltz, there's laughs to bloom.

You steal my fries, and I pout for fun,
Claiming my portion, 'Hey! Leave me none!'
In every moment, there's teasing, it's true,
Though your laughter's a treasure, I can't resist too.

Late-night giggles while the world is hushed,
Sharing confessions, our worries brushed.
A fleeting touch, a wink here and there,
A friendship that's wild, a bond we share.

So here's to the quirks in our tangled space,
Where eyes meet in silence, a warm embrace.
With every joke and every clap,
Life's just more fun when we both overlap.

The Quiet Strain of Togetherness

You're in your corner, I'm on a spree,
Too close for comfort, yet still so free.
Our inside jokes, an intricate web,
In this cozy chaos, we both ebb.

The remote stays missing, what a surprise!
You swear it's me; I roll my eyes.
In the tide of noise, with bickering bold,
We find moments sparkly, a treasure to hold.

Dinner disasters become our lore,
With burnt offerings at the kitchen door.
You mock my cooking, but I laugh and grin,
Knowing at heart, we both enjoy the din.

In these muted strains of our shared campaign,
Life's funny moments, through every vein.
Deftly we navigate this quirky tether,
In the quiet strain, we thrive together.

Solace Amidst Company

In a house full of voices, I seek my own,
While others share tales, I text on my phone.
The cat gives me judgment, it's hard to ignore,
Yet still I can hear them, through the closed door.

The kitchen's a circus, pots clang and race,
I sneak my own snacks, their recipes a chase.
Laughter erupts; I chuckle to myself,
While they appeal to me, I'll stick with my shelf.

I'm lost in their chaos, yet not quite alone,
Dodging their questions, like running from drones.
With a grin at the mayhem, I sip from my cup,
While they try to bond, I'm just coiled up.

Together but distant, we dance in the space,
Amidst all the voices, I find my own pace.
As they wrestle for connection, I giggle and scoot,
In this quirky ensemble, I'm still resolute.

The Echo of Us

In the living room bickering, the TV blares loud,
While I hide in the corner, a very proud crowd.
They argue the rules of a game I don't play,
I smile in my snuggles, pretending I'm gray.

As pancakes fly up, the syrup does too,
Each breakfast a battle, can I have some stew?
They gather round tables, enthralled by the fight,
While I plot my escape with a book on the side.

Oh, the sound of their laughter is like a nice tune,
But I savor my silence like eating a prune.
Their plans for a movie, I'd rather not see,
Instead, I'll binge-watch my best friend, TV.

Every room has its echo, some quiet, some loud,
Finding joy in the ruckus, I dance with the crowd.
While they're entangled, I sneak in one jest,
Living our lives, yet I'm still at my best.

Stolen Moments of Togetherness

Dining table chaos, forks jabbing with cheer,
While I play the sly thief, sneaking bites near.
They pass on the gossip, a feast for the tongue,
Yet I'm crafting my stories, and that's how I've sung.

In every loud sigh, there's a whisper of fun,
Where laughter erupts like a well-chosen pun.
At games night they bicker, the score going "whoa!"
I chuckle in silence, as knowledge they throw.

When togetherness beckons, I plot a retreat,
To nap on the sofa and savor my sweet.
Their plans for a movie? A snooze fest for sure,
I chuckle at midnight—solace so pure.

Yet when they come looking, I join in the fray,
With role as a jester, I'll bask in their play.
For in these small moments, I treasure my part,
Together yet scattered, it's quite the fine art.

Constrained Affections

In crowded rooms filled, there's a fight for the air,
While I wander like Fido, unaware of the flare.
A hug from my brother, just sideways and stilted,
And their laughs shimmer forth, my patience is tilted.

They share all their secrets, but I can't make sense,
Trapped in their chatter, it's quite the suspense.
I smile through the noise, a grimace or two,
While plotting my exit to sneak off for a brew.

Amid hastily made plans, I drift like a breeze,
Quietly freezing amidst all the tease.
While they woo and they fan, I search for the door,
In smiles and confusion, I'm yearning for more.

Yet, intertwined awkwardly in this big happy mess,
We navigate chaos, a loving duress.
In moments of laughter, my heart flops and pings,
We're all just a little bit strange, or so it seems.

When Touch Turns into Space

You reach for the snack, but it's too far,
The couch is a river, and you're a star.
Distance defined by a blanket or two,
Touching the remote is a workout for you.

Midnight cravings can't be shared, oh dear,
I'll just slide a note, let's keep it clear.
Your laughter bounces off walls, a ping,
While I silently wonder what snacks you bring.

A hug turns to a dance, a funny ballet,
Greeted by pillows, we sway and sway.
Our feet are so close, yet I can't quite feel,
The connection we search, just doesn't seem real.

Yet in this odd waltz, hilarity blooms,
Love's a comedy show played in each room.
So here we remain, a peculiar pair,
Where distance is heart, but laughs fill the air.

The Unseen Chasm

We share a wall, but it's quite a feat,
To send you a text, just to say 'Hi, sweet!'
Your side of the room, a mysterious land,
With snacks I can't reach, and pillows unplanned.

I tell you a joke, it travels a mile,
The laughter drifts slowly; I can see your smile.
You mix up the laundry, oh what a spree!
The colors of life living wild and free.

In pajamas we wander, both looking unique,
You're in a turtleneck, but I'm in my sleek.
We can wave from a distance, and seal it with cheer,
Just a sneeze away from an unexpected near.

Yet this invisible gap brings layers of fun,
Like two stars apart, we're still shining one.
With each chuckle and chuck, our bond grows anew,
In this game of space, it's just me and you.

Muffled Laughter in Separate Rooms

Your side has a pet, mine has a chair,
Muffled laughter floats, dances in the air.
I ask if you're winning, you say, 'Sort of, yes!'
While I'm in a contest of couch-potato-guess.

With cushions in place, we plan our attacks,
Yet you leave your socks, and I hide the snacks.
Echoes of jokes get lost in the hall,
But your mysterious giggles invite me to call.

I think I can hear your latest great pun,
While I'm sipping tea, pretending it's fun.
Both cracking up silent, it's a curious plot,
A duel in the living room — who'll take the shot?

Yet in this strange game, joyous chaos reigns,
We each hold our ground, knowing there are gains.
With laughter our bridge, no distance can sever,
We're neighbors in heart, always joined together.

Hearts that Share a Ceiling

Two hearts in this space, both vibrant and bright,
Our home's a circus, a comedy night.
With jokes through the halls, we toss them around,
A knock on the door, "Hey, did you hear the sound?"

I'll trade you a wink for a slice of that pie,
You clap as I juggle, and oh, how I try!
Your side has the flair, mine holds the charm,
Together we twinkle, a mystical calm.

Though miles may divide us, it's just one thin floor,
A ceiling above keeps us laughing for sure.
Each giggle reverberates, like magic it twirls,
Creating a tapestry of our daily swirls.

In this delightful dance, we stumble and sway,
Finding laughter together, in our quirky ballet.
So toast with your coffee, I'll cheer with my tea,
For in our own world, you're the best part of me.

Divergent Paths

We share a fridge, a couch, a TV,
Yet argue who took the last cold sweet tea.
I walk left, you stroll right, it's unclear,
How we still laugh at these quirks, my dear.

Our socks collide in the laundry room,
You leave dishes, I leave a broom.
You snore like a bear, it's quite the show,
I dream of silence, oh where did it go?

The dog stares, caught in our little feud,
Between cuddles and battles, he's so confused.
Matching pajamas, yet we can't agree,
On pizza toppings or what film to see.

Together in chaos, our lives interlace,
In a comedy sketch, our home is the place.
With silly disputes in this happy space,
We stand, side by side, in our funny race.

Close Yet Far

In one room, I play music too loud,
While you're trying to nap, oh sweet shroud.
With walls that can't hold our laughter tight,
We swing from banter to playful fight.

The popcorn flies as the movie unfolds,
Who knew fun fights could come with such bolds?
Your side's the cinema, mine's just a mess,
In this round of home, I must confess.

We linger near, yet worlds apart,
You chase the quiet while I stir the heart.
The remote is a treasure, a battle of wills,
A game of control, amidst comedic thrills.

Our hearts are linked, with humor as glue,
In this grand stage, it's me and it's you.
We twirl in the light of the hallway so bright,
Close yet far, in our playful plight.

Underneath the Surface

Beneath our banter, a river flows deep,
A treasure of giggles, where secrets keep.
We trade silly jests in the dead of night,
While pretending to sleep, pillow fight!

Your quirks are a charm, crazy but sweet,
From losing your keys to dancing on feet.
A mystery wrapped in a brilliant disguise,
Even your clumsiness is a surprise.

When dinner's a fuss, we'll laugh it away,
Whisking the soup, it turns out to play.
From burnt garlic bread to the pie that won't set,
Each culinary mess, we'll never regret.

We may be a duo that dances apart,
Yet stitched through the seams, there's love at the heart.
In laughter's warm glow, we bravely dive deep,
Illusions of danger, where we find our leap.

The Weight of Us

Two backpacks clash in the hall, we collide,
Each carrying baggage, our own foolish pride.
You shout "My spot!" I wave "Not today!"
In this travel of life, we journey our way.

Flatulent laughter from culinary quests,
As we whip up magic that fails the tests.
"Whose turn is it to do dishes tonight?"
We spar like two knights in a comical fight.

With TikTok dances that turn into flops,
We laugh at the madness as joy never stops.
In the weight of it all, we find lightness, too,
With each silly moment, I cherish you.

The chaos we share may not seem just right,
But together we shine, a bright, silly light.
In the loving discord, we gladly exist,
One roof, two souls, woven in a twist.

www.ingramcontent.com/pod-product-compliance
Lightning Source LLC
Chambersburg PA
CBHW060112230426
43661CB00003B/165